Erosion and Weathering

WELDON OWEN PTY LTD

Publisher: Sheena Coupe
Senior Designer: Kylie Mulquin
Editorial Coordinators: Sarah Anderson,
Tracey Gibson
Production Manager: Helen Creeke
Production Assistant: Kylie Lawson

Project Editor: Ariana Klepac
Designer: Patricia Ansell
Text: Jan Stradling

05 04 03 02
10 9 8 7 6 5 4 3 2

Published in the United States by
Wright Group/McGraw-Hill
19201 120th Avenue NE, Suite 100
Bothell, WA 98011
www.WrightGroup.com

Printed in Singapore
ISBN: 0-7699-1234-6

CREDITS AND ACKNOWLEDGMENTS

PICTURE AND ILLUSTRATION CREDITS
[t=top, b=bottom, l=left, r=right, c=center]
Corbis 9br, 13tl. **Corel Corporation** 1c, 6b, 7b, 8t, 9tl, 11t, 15b, 16b, 21t, 23c. **Chris Forsey** 5b, 12–13, 15t, 18–19b, 24.
Mike Lamble 19t. **Photodisc** 10b, 11b, 14bc, 23tr. **PhotoEssentials** banding; **Sandra Pond/Wildlife Art Ltd.** 7t. **Trevor Ruth** 22.
Claudia Saraceni 20. **Michael Saunders** 3, 4–5t, 17, 21b.

Weldon Owen would like to thank the following people for their assistance in the production of this book:
Peta Gorman, Michael Hann, Marney Richardson.

Contents

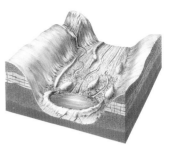

Erosion and Weathering

Erosion happens when rivers, oceans, ice, and wind change the Earth's shape. Weather and growing plants can crack and split the Earth's surface. This is called *weathering*.

Cracking Up

1. Roll some clay into a ball.
   Wet the ball and wrap in plastic.
2. Place in the freezer overnight.
   The next day the clay will be
   cracked like frozen earth.

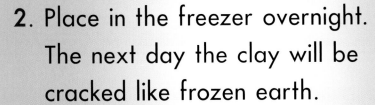

Mountains and Valleys

The Earth has plates of rock under the surface. When two plates push together they form mountains. Valleys are the parts between two mountains.

Valley

Worn Away

1. Fill a tray with sand and raise one end.
2. Spray a gentle stream of water into the tray.
3. As the water runs off, a valley will form in the sand.

Mountains

Wide river valley

Rivers

Water flows from mountaintops to form rivers. Huge slabs of ice called *glaciers* can melt and become rivers. Rivers change the shape of the land as they move across it.

A river erodes the Earth as it runs through steep valleys.

A river delta happens where the river meets the ocean.

Lakes and Craters

Sometimes water from rivers, rain, and mountain springs fills holes or *craters* in the ground to form lakes. Some craters are caused by volcanoes or *meteorites.*

Meteorite crater

Alpine lake

Volcanic crater lake

Coastlines

The *coastline* is always changing shape. The wind and water batter cliff faces. Sand dunes form when the wind blows the sand around and piles it up.

Cliffs Sea cliffs Arch Sea stack Blowhole

The ocean is slowly eroding the rock under these houses.

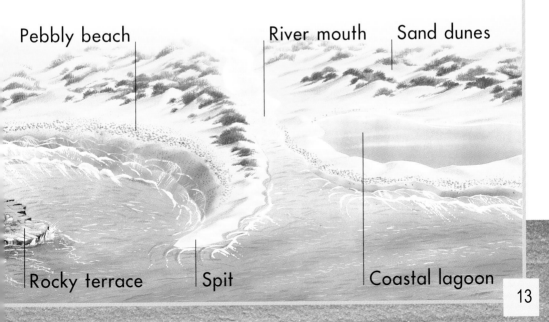

Pebbly beach

River mouth

Sand dunes

Rocky terrace

Spit

Coastal lagoon

Sea Caves and Stacks

The wind and waves are very strong. They *carve* caves and sea stacks out of cliff faces. Sea stacks were once joined to cliffs.

Sea caves are carved out of the shoreline by waves.

Waves hit the cliffs every day. Caves shaped like arches begin to form. The arches get bigger until the top falls off and a sea stack is formed.

Sea stacks

Canyons and Hoodoos

Over a long time water erodes rock
to form all sorts of amazing shapes.
Canyons and hoodoos are formed
by water erosion.

Canyon de Chelly, Arizona

Canyons

Rivers cut into rock
to make deep valleys.
When the valley becomes
very wide, a canyon
is formed.

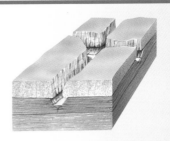

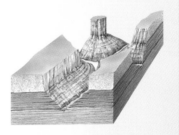

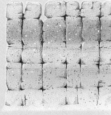

Hoodoos

Cracks appear when water
seeps into rock and freezes.
The cracks become wider
and columns called hoodoos
are formed.

Volcanic Landforms

Volcanoes change the land around them. New craters are formed with each explosion. Layers of *lava* build up to make *plateaus.*

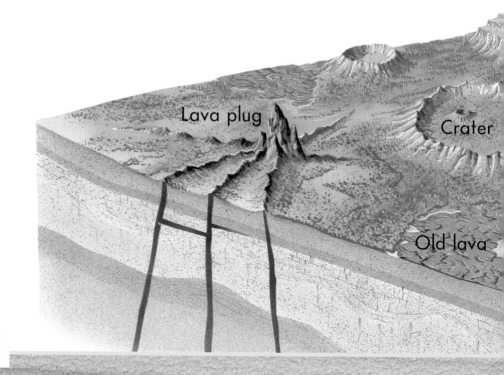

Lava plug

Crater

Old lava

In Turkey, some people live in houses cut into soft volcanic rock.

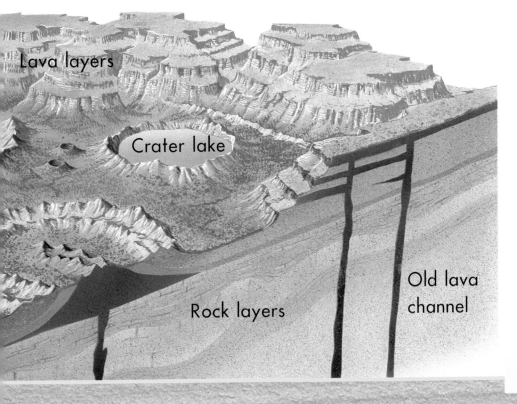

Lava layers

Crater lake

Old lava channel

Rock layers

Experts who study glaciers are called glaciologists.

Glaciers

Glaciers are giant rivers of ice. As the ice slides downward, it cuts a U-shaped valley into the mountain. It slices at the Earth as it goes by.

Glacier breaking up

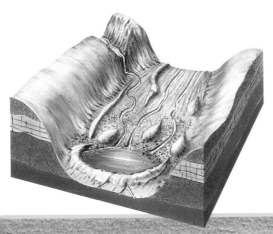

A U-shaped valley is left when a glacier melts away.

Plants stop sand dunes from blowing away.

Erosion

Plant roots help keep soil in place. When soil is no longer protected, cleared areas erode quickly.

Without plants
the wind
can blow
soil away.

It is important to care for
the world's rain forests.

Glossary

carve To shape by cutting.

coastline The rocks, cliffs, and sand dunes along a seashore.

crater A bowl-shaped hole.

glacier A huge slab of ice moving slowly down a mountain or valley.

lava Hot liquid rock that comes out of a volcano.

meteorite A lump of rock that falls to Earth from space.

plateau A flat area.

weathering When rocks are broken down by plant roots or harsh weather.

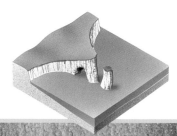